The World of Mythology:
Japanese Mythology

By Jim Ollhoff

VISIT US AT
WWW.ABDOPUBLISHING.COM

Published by ABDO Publishing Company, 8000 West 78th Street, Suite 310, Edina, MN 55439.

Printed in the United States of America, North Mankato, Minnesota.
022011
092011

 PRINTED ON RECYCLED PAPER

Editor: John Hamilton
Graphic Design: Sue Hamilton
Cover Design: Neil Klinepier
Cover Photo: Gonzalo Ordóñez
Interior Photos and Illustrations: Alamy-pgs 14, 20 & 21; AP-pgs 5 & 10; CaptainMaz-pg 28; CIA-pg 6; Corbis-pgs 15, 17, 19 & 23; Eitaku Kobayashi-pg 13; Getty Images-pgs 11 & 27; Glow Images-pg 29; iStockphoto-border graphic; Jade Sheldon-pg 26; Library of Congress-pgs 7, 22, 24, 25, 28, 29 & 32; NASA-pg 12; Thinkstock-pgs 4, 18 & 31; Tsukioka Yoshitoshi-pg 16; Yashima Gukutei-pg 26.

Library of Congress Cataloging-in-Publication Data

Ollhoff, Jim, 1959-
  Japanese mythology / Jim Ollhoff.
     p. cm. -- (The world of mythology)
  Includes index.
  ISBN 978-1-61714-723-4
  1. Mythology, Japanese--Juvenile literature. I. Title.
  BL2203.O45 2011
  398.20952--dc22
                                      2010042019

CONTENTS

THE MIGHTY MYTH

The world can be a confusing place. People who are close to us get sick or die. People who are evil get positions of power and wealth. Things don't work the way we want them to, and we have a hard time understanding life. We need help to make sense of the world.

Art, music, drama, and poetry have helped us make the world a little less confusing. These things can give comfort, guidance, inspiration, or new insights. Down through the years of human history, mythology has helped people make sense of life. Stories about how the gods behaved have helped people understand relationships. Stories of heroic journeys have inspired people to go on travels of their own. Myths have helped people live with more meaning, inspiration, and intensity.

Mythology has always been important to the people of Japan. Even today, Japanese mythology is expressed in art, literature, and dance. Japanese people still learn to tell their ancient stories and myths.

Art, music, drama, and poetry let us use our imagination. Mythology also lets our imaginations run free.

Right: Art, music, drama, and poetry allow people to tell stories and use their imaginations.

Above: Japanese people tell stories and myths through traditional performances.

LAND OF THE RISING SUN

The word *Japan* means "sun origin." This is why Japan is sometimes called the "Land of the Rising Sun." Japan consists of four main islands and many smaller islands. The Sea of Japan separates mainland China from the islands of Japan.

Historians aren't sure when people first arrived in Japan. The first people may have come as early as 30,000 BC. Early Japanese people lived as hunters and gatherers. Archeologists have found many fertility statues in Japan. Ancient peoples believed that fertility gods would make their food crops grow. By 250 BC, people were beginning to grow rice in irrigated fields, make more advanced pottery, and weave garments.

Local Japanese governments began to emerge. The history of Japan is scarred with civil wars between various warlords. Many clans and military leaders tried to unify Japan under a single government. A final, permanently united Japan didn't come about until the early 1600s.

Right: A modern map of Japan.

Japan is known as the "Land of the Rising Sun."

THE SOUL OF JAPAN

A Japanese Dogu statue from the 4th century BC. It may have been a spirit of healing or a guide for the dead.

There is no written record of the earliest people of Japan. Archeologists have found pottery, stones that seem to have special significance, and statues of gods and goddesses. The earliest Japanese people probably had folk religions like most other cultures, including beliefs in sky gods, weather gods, and agricultural gods.

Then, about 500 BC, a religion called Shinto began to emerge. Shinto had no leader, no first prophet, and no sacred writings. It emerged from all of the folk religions, and became a loose collection of beliefs and ideas about the spiritual world. Shinto had few organized beliefs about the afterlife. Shinto became very influential on the mythology of Japan.

The word Shinto means "the way of the gods." One of the important beliefs of Shinto was that everything has a god attached to it. There were deities for mountains, foods, families, trees, rocks, rivers, and everything else. These gods, called Kami, were generally helpful to people. Sometimes the word "Kami" meant not individual gods, but rather the spiritual force of all the gods. Many Shinto believers thought of themselves as "children of the Kami." This meant that everyone and everything was sacred.

Above: A painting of a Shinto Shrine in Ise, Japan, created in the late 1500s.

Shinto also honored ancestors. Even today, many Japanese have small altars in their homes dedicated to their ancestors. Huge Shinto altars, called shrines, have been built all over Japan. Many people still attend the Shinto shrines for prayers, dances, and other rituals during important life events.

Japanese mythology tells stories about creation, the start of the emperor, and other topics. It is a blend of concepts from Shinto, ancient folk religions, and parts of stories borrowed from Chinese mythology. The Japanese myths are long stories of fantastic creatures and supernatural beings. Like myths from around the world, the Japanese stories are sometimes funny, sometimes sad, but always exciting.

Above: A torii gate is often the entrance to a Shinto shrine. Crossing through it represents going from the ungodly to the sacred.

Above: A woman and her son pray by a Shinto shrine in Japan.

The Japanese Creation Story

According to Japanese mythology, the Earth began as a floating ooze. Five gods appeared. They were called the "Separate Heavenly Deities." These gods gave birth to other gods and goddesses for several generations. Finally, the gods gave birth to two people: a man, Izanagi, and a woman, Izanami.

The gods told Izanagi and Izanami to make dry land appear from the ooze. So, they stood on a bridge in heaven. They stirred the oozy waters with a jeweled spear. When they took the spear out of the ooze, droplets fell back onto the water, forming an island called Onogoro. This mythical island was the start of the world.

Izanagi and Izanami built a palace on the island, and then decided to get married. They performed the ritual of marriage, but their first child was a terrible monster. They asked the gods what happened. The gods replied that they had performed the marriage ritual out of order. Izanagi and Izanami performed their marriage ritual again. Izanami began to have many children, and the children became the islands of Japan and the Kami—the gods of the mountains, rivers, and everything else.

Myth says that Izanagi and Izanami's children became the islands of Japan.

Left: Izanagi (man) and Izanami (woman) stir the ooze with a jeweled spear to make dry land appear. A painting by Eitaku Kobayashi, circa 1885.

Izanami's last child was the fire god. The fire burned Izanami so badly that she died. Her heartbroken husband, Izanagi, decided to go to the underworld to see if he could bring back his wife. They met in the underworld, although it was completely dark and he couldn't see her. She told him that she would find out if she could leave, but in the meantime, he must not look at her face.

Izanami's last child was Kagu-tsuchi, the fire god. Izanami died giving birth to him.

But the mournful Izanagi wanted to see her face, so he lit a torch. To his horror, he saw that she was decomposed and covered with maggots. He turned and ran. Furious, she sent demons after him. Izanagi put a large stone in front of the entrance of the underworld so the demons couldn't escape. Izanami told her husband that she was so angry that she would introduce death into the world. Izanagi told her that he would bring more life into the world than she could bring death.

Izanagi wanted to wash himself off after his underworld trip, so he stopped in a stream and took off his clothing. Three gods emerged from his clothing: Amaterasu, the sun goddess; Tsuki-yomi, the moon god; and Susano, the ocean god.

Above: The Myoto-Iwa, or Wedded Rocks, just off the Japanese coast in Ise Bay. The rocks symbolize Izanagi and Izanami, the male and female deites who created Japan. The larger rock, the male Izanagi, has a torii gate on top.

AMATERASU, THE SUN GODDESS

materasu, the sun goddess, was happy to rule the heavens. However, her brother, Susano, didn't want to rule the oceans. He thought it was a lesser job than governing the heavens. Susano and Amaterasu had an argument about who was greater.

Different versions of the myth tell us different things about what happened next. One version says that they had a contest to see who could create more deities. Amaterasu ate Susano's sword and spit out three gods. Susano stole her necklace and turned them into more gods. The argument got worse and worse, with Susano destroying temples and rice fields. Finally, Amaterasu had to run away and hide. With the sun goddess in hiding, the Earth was plunged into darkness. Evil spirits and demons emerged from the darkness to make matters worse.

The other gods finally coaxed Amaterasu out of hiding and punished Susano. Amaterasu became one of the most popular gods of Japan. She was the ancestor of Jimmu, the mythological first emperor of Japan. The royal family of Japan still uses the sword and necklace of Amaterasu as symbols.

Right: Jimmu, the mythical first emperor of Japan.

大日本名将鑑

天照皇大神天の巌戸に隠れまさせたまひ世の中常暗のごとくなれば八百萬の神たち巌戸の前に集ひ神いさめの神楽を奏し百女命舞ひたまふに天鈿女命のしなひ扉を少し開きみたまひて手力雄命其扉を取り投うちやりやの多なる女神ら遠くに飛びて信に止るより戸隠明神と申し奉る

Above: Amaterasu the sun goddess hid in a cave, plunging the Earth into darkness.

How O-Kuni-Nushi Got a Wife

O-kuni-nushi was the god of medicine. One day, O-kuni-nushi saw a wounded rabbit, and stopped to help the animal. The rabbit was actually a god in disguise. As a reward for his kind deed, the rabbit gave him permission to marry the daughter of the god Susano.

Susano, however, was not so sure about O-kuni-nushi. He told O-kuni-nushi that he would have to perform a series of tasks to earn the right to marry his daughter. Susano, who was an unpredictable and sometimes evil god, made the tasks very gruesome. He made O-kuni-nushi sleep in a room full of poisonous insects, and then placed him in a room full of snakes. To help O-kuni-nushi survive the tasks, his bride-to-be gave him an enchanted scarf for protection. As O-kuni-nushi's final test, Susano started a large fire around him. However, O-kuni-nushi was saved by a friendly mouse, who led him to safety.

A mouse helped O-kuni-nushi.

O-kuni-nushi completed all the tasks, but was angry at Susano. O-kuni-nushi tied Susano's long hair to the wooden beams in the ceiling, and then took Susano's magic bow and harp. Susano started to respect O-kuni-nushi, and gave him permission to marry his daughter.

Above: A statue of O-kuni-nushi and the god disguised as a wounded rabbit.

Jimmu, The First Emperor

materasu, the sun goddess, had many children. Her great-great-great grandson was Jimmu, the mythical first emperor of Japan. Even though dates are sometimes given for his reign, most historians don't believe that Jimmu actually existed. Japanese emperors often claimed to be divine. The myth of Jimmu allowed them to trace their families back to divine origins, all the way back to Amaterasu.

It was said that Jimmu was a fierce warrior who was guided by a deity in the shape of a crow. He marched with his army to take large areas of Japan, defeating many deities along the way. At one point, Jimmu's army was poisoned by the enemy's gods. However, Amaterasu gave Jimmu a magic sword in order to defeat his enemies.

Above: A deity in the shape of a crow guided Jimmu.

Above: Jimmu, the mythical first emperor, marched with his army to take large areas of Japan, defeating many deities along the way.

THE ONI: JAPANESE DEVILS

The Shinto underworld was called Jigoku. There, the ruler of the underworld judged the souls of the dead. The demons of the underworld were called Oni. The Oni lived in the underworld, but also on the Earth. They created much trouble and misery for people. They were responsible for death and disease, as well as crop failure in the fields. Sometimes they stole people's souls.

The Oni were usually invisible, but people who were very good, kind, and upright could sometimes see the Oni. The Oni were not very intelligent, and so their evil plans were often stopped. One of the main gods who stopped the Oni was named Shoki the Demon Queller. Shoki protected people from the mischief of the Oni. The Oni were frightened of Shoki, and so he could easily scare them away. It was common in Japan to hang a picture of Shoki outside one's door to scare away the Oni.

Right: A Japanese demon, or Oni, hangs on a pillar as a sword pokes up from below.

Above: Shoki the Demon Queller protected people from the mischief of the Oni.

HEROES

Similar to Chinese mythology, Japan had human heroes who did very brave things, and so sometimes were awarded the status of gods.

Ojin: Ojin was said to be an early emperor of Japan. He brought writing to the people, and cultural exchange with China and Korea. A wise leader, he was later identified as the god of war.

Kintaro: Kintaro was a boy who was incredibly strong. There are many stories about his accomplishments, including one story where he pulled a tree out of the ground to kill a giant, evil spider.

Left: Raiko, a famous warrior, fights the Oe Mountain demon, Shutendoji.

Raiko: Raiko was a warrior who became famous for fighting monsters. He came upon an evil giant who drank human blood. Raiko dressed up as a priest in order to sneak into the giant's fort. Raiko drugged the giant's bodyguards, and then killed the giant.

POPULAR JAPANESE GODS AND GODDESSES

Japanese gods and goddesses were powerful and honorable. They helped people in their day-to-day lives, as well as protected the country of Japan.

Amaterasu: The most important goddess in Japanese mythology. She ruled the heavens and was the ancestor of the Japanese emperors.

Benten: The goddess of music, wealth, love, and good luck. She was very shy, but married a large, ugly dragon. She married the dragon even though he was very ugly, and this showed that she was very good and honorable. This act brought peace to Japan.

Ninigi: The grandson of Amaterasu. He went down to Earth to defeat the sons of the sorcerer-god, who were cutthroat thieves. He also showed people how to plant rice.

Inari: The rice god, and the protector of farmers. Because rice is such an important crop in Japan, Inari was a much-loved god. Many villages still have Shinto shrines dedicated to Inari. He is often pictured as an old man carrying a sack of rice.

Hachiman: The Shinto war god, who is sometimes identified with Ojin, one of the early emperors of Japan. He is considered the protector of Japan.

Susano: The storm god, he was the brother of Amaterasu. He is known for creating disorder, first by becoming jealous of Amaterasu. He was so angry at Amaterasu that he began to destroy the world, and was finally banished from heaven. He had adventures after that, such as rescuing a kingdom from an eight-headed dragon.

Ryujin (above): The dragon-king of the sea. He was an important ocean god. He had an enormous mouth, which he used to control the ebb and flow of the tides.

The Seven Gods of Fortune (left): These were a group of seven gods, responsible for things like long life, generosity, wealth, work, and other ways to become fortunate. Two of these gods seem to have originated in Japan. The rest may have been borrowed from China, and perhaps India.

GLOSSARY

DEITY

A god or supreme being.

DOGU STATUE

A statue made in the general shape of a human or animal. These figurines were produced in prehistoric Japan around 14,000 BC to 400 BC. They were belived to have been used in religious or fertility rituals.

EMPEROR

The ruler of Japan.

FERTILITY GODS

Gods associated with the ability of humans to have children, as well as pregnancy and birth.

JIGOKU

The Shinto underworld.

JIMMU

The mythological first emperor of Japan. According to legend, Jimmu was the sun goddess Ameratsu's great-great-great grandson. It is said that Jimmu was born in 711 BC and died in 585 BC. However, most historians do not believe Jimmu ever lived.

KAMI

The gods that inhabit everything.

ONI

Evil spirits, usually invisible, who bring trouble upon people.

SACRED

Someone or something that is said to be holy or blessed. The person or object usually has a religious connection to a god or gods.

SHINTO

An important religion in Japan.

TORII GATE

A gateway to a Japanese Shinto shrine or temple. The torii gate has two upright posts supporting two crosspieces. Crossing through the torii gate represents moving from the ungodly to the sacred.

Left: An illustration of a torii gate.

INDEX

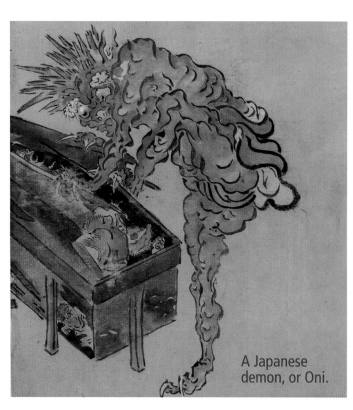

A Japanese demon, or Oni.